Languages of the World

Japanese

Harriet Milles

www.raintreepublishers.co.uk
Visit our website to find out
more information about
Raintree books.

To order:
☎ Phone 0845 6044371
🖨 Fax +44 (0) 1865 312263
🖳 Email myorders@raintreepublishers.co.uk

Customers from outside the UK please telephone +44 1865 312262

Raintree is an imprint of Capstone Global Library Limited,
a company incorporated in England and Wales having its
registered office at 7 Pilgrim Street, London, EC4V 6LB –
Registered company number: 6695582

Text © Capstone Global Library Limited 2012
First published in hardback in 2012
Paperback edition first published in 2013
The moral rights of the proprietor have been asserted.

Edited by Dan Nunn and Diyan Leake
Designed by Marcus Bell
Original illustrations © Capstone Global Library Ltd 2012
Picture research by Elizabeth Alexander
Originated by Capstone Global Library Ltd
Printed and bound in China by South China Printing
 Company Ltd

ISBN 978 1 406 23284 4 (hardback)
15 14 13 12 11
10 9 8 7 6 5 4 3 2 1

ISBN 978 1 406 23291 2 (paperback)
16 15 14 13 12
10 9 8 7 6 5 4 3 2 1

British Library Cataloguing in Publication Data
Milles, Harriet.
  Japanese. -- (Languages of the world)
  495.6-dc22
A full catalogue record for this book is available from the
British Library.

Acknowledgements
The author and publisher are grateful to the following for
permission to reproduce copyright material: Alamy pp. 5
(© Alex Segre), 6 (© Photo Resource Hawaii), 13 (© amana
images inc.), 22 (© John Cole), 23 (© amana images inc.);
Getty Images pp. 8 (MIXA), 21 (MIXA); iStockphoto pp. 7
(© Stephan Hoerold), 16 (© Christine Glade); Photolibrary
pp. 18 (Klaus-Werner Friedrich), 24 (JTB Photo); Shutterstock
pp. 9 (© discpicture), 11 (© Mandy Godbehear), 12 (© grafica),
14 (© mamahoohooba), 15 (© AVAVA), 17 (© paulaphoto),
19 (© Steve Yager), 20 (© Monkey Business Images), 25 (© J.
Henning Buchholz), 26 (© bonchan), 27 (© svry), 28 (© Jose
AS Reyes), 29 (© takayuki).

Cover photograph reproduced with permission of Alamy
(© MIXA).

Every effort has been made to contact copyright holders of
material reproduced in this book. Any omissions will be
rectified in subsequent printings if notice is given to the
publisher.

Contents

Japanese words in this book are in italics, *like this*.
You can find out how to say them by looking in the
pronunciation guide.

What do you know about Japanese?

Japanese is the language of the country of Japan, in Asia. Japanese people call their country *Nippon*, which means "Land of the Rising Sun". They call their language *Nihongo*.

Japan is a country of four main islands and many smaller islands.

Japan

This is a busy street in Tokyo. Tokyo is the capital city of Japan.

Politeness is very important in Japan. Children speak differently to adults than to their friends. People speak differently at work than at home.

Who speaks Japanese?

Japan is the only country in the world where Japanese is the main language. Many Japanese-speaking people live in Hawaii in the United States.

Some people born in Hawaii have Japanese parents or grandparents.

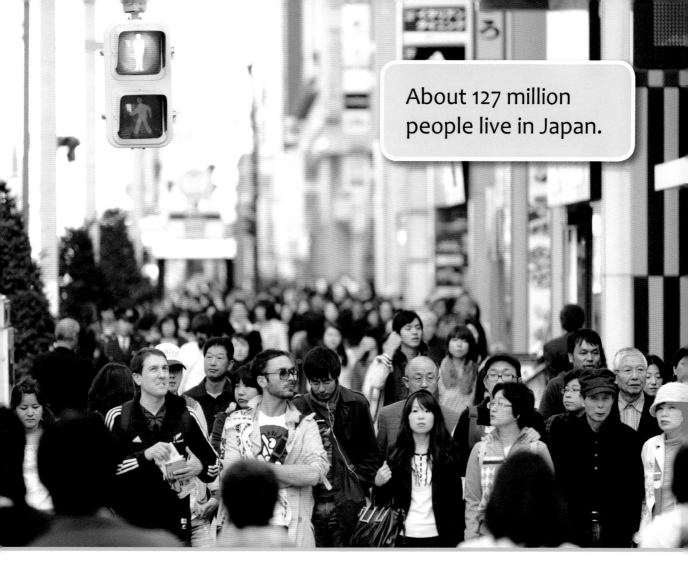

About 127 million people live in Japan.

There are also Japanese-speaking people in Brazil and Peru in South America. Japanese is fun to learn! Are you ready to speak some Japanese?

Reading and writing in Japanese

Japanese people write in "characters", or scripts. They use three different reading and writing systems. *Kanji* and *hiragana* are the most commonly used systems.

Japanese children must learn to read and write 1,006 characters before they leave primary school!

私　*kanji*

わたし　*hiragana*

ワタシ　*katakana*

Here is the Japanese word for "I" (*watashi*) written in the different scripts.

Katakana is mostly used for names and non-Japanese words. Japanese characters can look difficult for English-speaking people. Don't worry! Turn the page to find an easy way to learn Japanese.

Learning Japanese

People who are learning Japanese for the first time will usually be taught in *romaji*. In *romaji*, Japanese words are written in the same alphabet that is used to write English.

Japanese character	Romaji	How to say it	English
山	yama	ya-ma	mountain
おいしい	oishii	oy-shee	nice, tasty
テレビ	terebi	te-re-bi	television

These are Japanese words that are written in letters of the English alphabet.

Romaji helps you to know how Japanese characters should sound. You may already know some *romaji*! If you or your friends go to *judo* or *karate* classes, you use Japanese words.

Saying hello and goodbye

Japanese people usually greet each other by bowing. They may say, "*Konnichiwa!*" to greet a friend, or "*Hajimemashite*" ("It's nice to meet you"), if they are meeting someone for the first time.

How to say it
hello = *konnichiwa*
It's nice to
    meet you =
    Hajimemashite

How to say it
goodbye (leaving for a long time) = *sayonara*
good morning = *ohayougozaimasu*
good evening = *konbanwa*
good night = *oyasuminasai*

The Japanese say, "*Moshi, moshi!*"
("Speak, speak!") when they answer
the telephone. There are different ways
to say goodbye. *Itte kimasu* means
"Goodbye, see you later."

Talking about yourself

When you meet people for the first time, they will usually ask for your name. Then you may say, "*Watashi no namae wa … desu*" ("My name is …").

How to say it
My name is Yuko = *Watashi no namae wa Yuko desu*

How to say it
I live in Tokyo = *Watashi wa Tokyo ni sunde imasu*
I come from Osaka = *Watashi wa Osaka kara kimashita*

They may ask you where you live. You can say, "*Watashi wa … ni sunde imasu*" ("I live in …"), or "*Watashi wa … kara kimashita*" ("I come from …").

Asking about others

If you want to ask someone's name, you can say, *"Anata no namae wa nan desu ka?"* ("What is your name?").

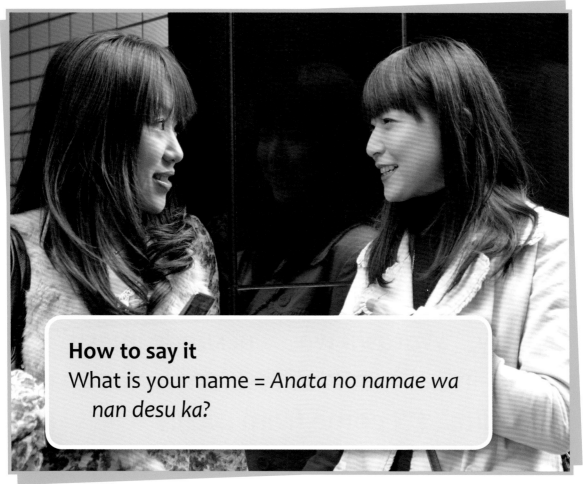

How to say it
What is your name = *Anata no namae wa nan desu ka?*

How to say it
Where are you from? = *Doko kara kimashita ka?*
Where do you live? = *Doko ni sunde imasu ka?*

To find out where someone comes from, you may say, *"Doko kara kimashita ka?"* ("Where are you from?"), or *"Doko ni sunde imasu ka?"* ("Where do you live?")

At home

Japanese homes usually have a kitchen, bathroom, toilet, and one or two rooms for living. People never wear shoes indoors. They take them off at the door.

How to say it
home = *uchi*
kitchen = *kitchin*
bathroom = *ofuro*
toilet = *toire*

How to say it
living room = *ima*
bed = *beddo* or *futon*

Traditional Japanese homes have mats called *tatami* on the floor. The family sit on cushions, not chairs. At night they sleep on the floor on special mattresses called *futon*.

Family

Japanese families are generally small, with just one or two children. Sometimes grandparents live with the family, too. In springtime, families go on picnics to enjoy the cherry blossom.

How to say it

family = *kazoku*

mother = *haha*

father = *chichi*

grandparents = *sofubo*

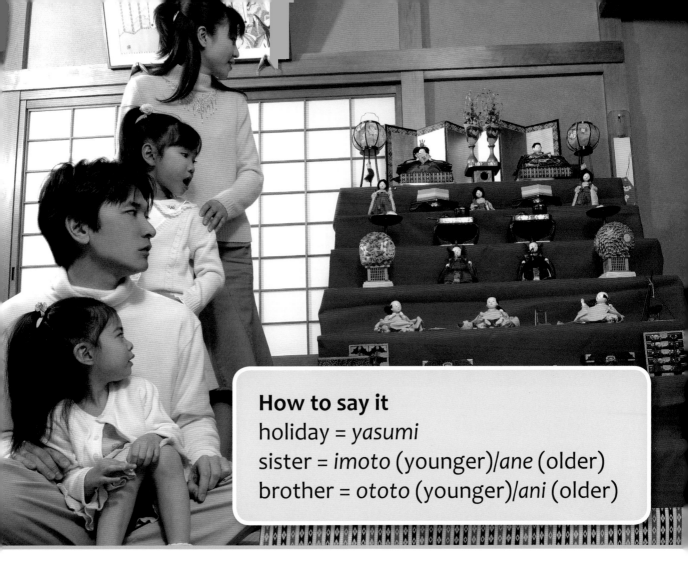

How to say it
holiday = *yasumi*
sister = *imoto* (younger)/*ane* (older)
brother = *ototo* (younger)/*ani* (older)

Families do things together on special festival days and holidays. On Children's Day (*Kodomo no hi*), boys fly kites shaped like fish. On Girls' Day (*Hina matsuri*), families display dolls.

21

At school

Japanese schools start at 8.30 a.m. and finish at around 4.00 p.m. Children learn how to read and write in the different types of Japanese characters. They also learn maths, history, and science.

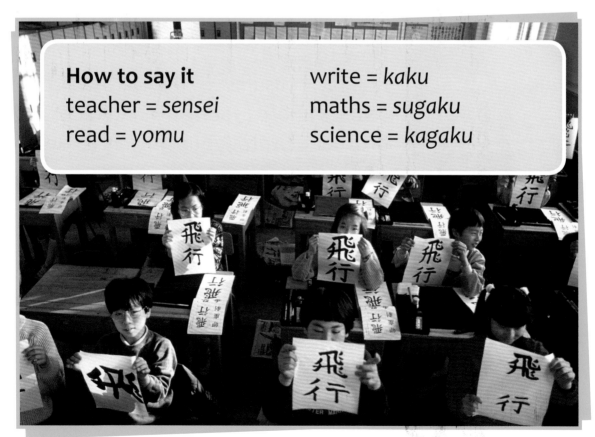

How to say it
teacher = *sensei*
read = *yomu*

write = *kaku*
maths = *sugaku*
science = *kagaku*

How to say it
class = *kurasu*
school = *gakko*
pupil = *seito*
learn = *manabu*
clean = *soujisuru*

After lunch, all the children clean the school. Then they may play sport or do other activities, such as music or dancing. They may have more classes, or a study period.

Sports and leisure

Japan is famous for martial arts. These are fighting sports, such as *judo*, *karate*, and *kendo*. Children in Japan start to learn one of these arts at a young age.

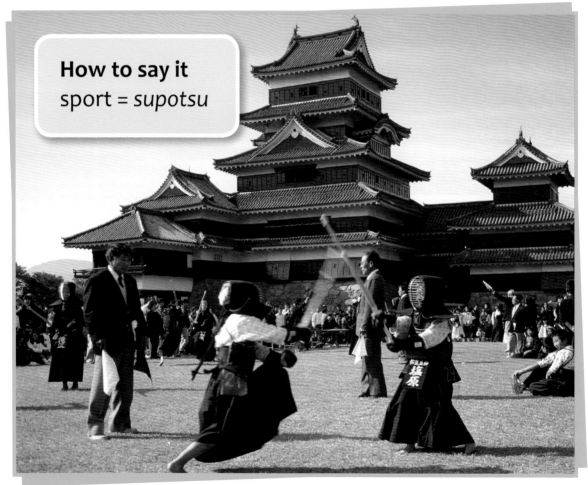

How to say it
sport = *supotsu*

How to say it
football = *sakka*
team = *chimu*
ball = *boru*

The national sport of Japan is sumo wrestling. Football, baseball, surfing, and skiing are also popular sports. In their free time, Japanese children love to read *manga* (comic books).

Food

Rice, noodles, and fish are popular foods in Japan. Breakfast may be a bowl of rice with soup and an egg, or some fish. All meals are eaten with chopsticks.

How to say it
rice = *gohan*
noodles = *men*
chopsticks = *o-hashi*

A popular lunchtime meal is noodles with vegetables, seaweed, and fish. A Japanese lunchbox is called a *bento*. Some shops sell ready-made *bento* for people to take away.

Clothes

Most Japanese people relax in T-shirts and jeans. They wear smarter clothes for work. People love colour in Japan! Some teenagers wear a brightly coloured style of clothes called *decora*.

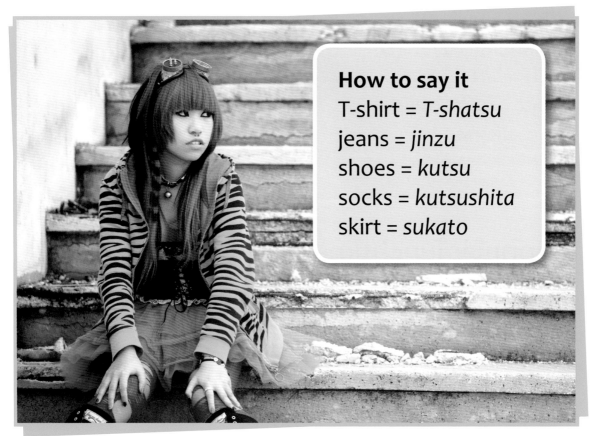

How to say it
T-shirt = *T-shatsu*
jeans = *jinzu*
shoes = *kutsu*
socks = *kutsushita*
skirt = *sukato*

People wear *kimono* with a wide sash called an *obi*.

For special occasions, people may dress in a traditional Japanese robe called a *kimono*. They will wear special sandals called *zori* on their feet.

Pronunciation guide

English	Romaji	Pronunciation
bathroom	ofuro	o-**fu**-ro
bed	beddo or futon	**bed**-do/fu-**ton**
breakfast	asa-gohan	a-**sa**-**go**-han
brother	ototo (younger)/ani (older)	o-**toh**-to/**a**-ni
chopsticks	o-hashi	o-**ha**-shi
class	kurasu	**ku**-ra-s
clean	souji-suru	**saw**-**ji**-su-ru
dinner	ban-gohan	ban-**go**-han
English	Eigo	**ay**-go
family	kazoku	**ka**-zo-ku
father	chichi	chi-**chi**
fish	sakana	sa-**ka**-**na**
football	sakka	**sak**-kah
good evening	konbanwa	kon-**ban**-wa
good morning	ohayougozaimasu	o-**ha**-**yoh**-go-zai-mas
good night	oyasuminasai	o-**ya**-su-**mi**-na-sai
goodbye	sayonara (for a long time)/ itte kimasu (leaving the house)	sa-**yoh**-**na**-ra/ it-**te ki**-ma-s
grandparents	sofubo	so-**fu**-bo
hello	konnichiwa	kon-**ni**-**chi**-wa
holiday	yasumi	ya-**su**-**mi**
home	uchi	ooh-**chi**
I come from …	Watashi wa … kara kimashita	wa-**ta**-**shi** wa … **ka**-ra ki-ma-**shi**-**ta**
I live in …	Watashi wa … ni sunde imasu	wa-**ta**-**shi** wa … ni **su**-n-de i-ma-s
It's nice to meet you	Hajimemashite	ha-**ji**-**me**-ma-**shi**-tih
Japanese	Nihongo	ni-**hon**-go
jeans	jinzu	**jee**-n-zu
kitchen	kitchin	**kit**-chin

learn	*manabu*	*ma-**na**-bu*
living room	*ima*	*i-**ma***
lunch	*hiru-gohan*	*hi-**ru**-**go**-han*
maths	*sugaku*	*su-**ga**-ku*
mother	*haha*	***ha**-ha*
My name is …	*Watashi no namae wa … desu*	*wa-**ta**-**shi** no na-**ma**-e wa … des*
noodles	*men*	***men***
please	*onegai shimasu*	*o-**ne-gai shi**-mas*
pupil	*seito*	***say**-to*
read	*yomu*	***yo**-mu*
rice	*gohan*	***go**-han*
school	*gakko*	*gak-**koh***
science	*kagaku*	***ka**-ga-ku*
shoes	*kutsu*	*ku-**tsu***
sister	*imoto (younger)/ane (older)*	*ih-**moh**-to/a-nih*
skirt	*sukato*	*su-**kah**-to*
socks	*kutsushita*	*ku-**tsu**-**shi**-ta*
sport	*supotsu*	*su-**poh**-ts*
T-shirt	*T-shatsu*	*T-**sha**-ts*
teacher	*sensei*	*sen-**say***
team	*chimu*	***chee**-mu*
thank you	*arigato gozaimasu*	*a-**ri**-ga-toh go-**zai**-mas*
toilet	*toire*	***toy**-re*
What does that mean?	*Kore wa nan to yuu imi desu ka?*	*ko-**re wa nan** to yuu i-mi des **ka***
What is your name?	*Anata no namae wa nan desu ka?*	*a-**na-ta** no na-**ma-e** wa **nan** des **ka***
Where are you from?	*Doko kara kimashita ka?*	***do**-ko ka-ra ki-**ma**-**shi**-ta **ka***
Where do you live?	*Doko ni sunde imasu ka?*	***do**-ko ni **su**-n-de i--mas **ka***
write	*kaku*	***ka**-ku*

1 = chi, 2 = ni, 3 = san, 4 = shi, 5 = go, 6 = roku, 7 = shichi, 8 = hachi, 9 = kyu, 10 = ju

Find out more

Books

I'm Learning Japanese!: A Language Adventure for Young People, Christian Galan and Florence Lerot-Calvo (Tuttle Shokai Inc., 2010)

Japan (National Geographic Countries of the World), Charles Phillips (National Geographic, 2009)

My First Japanese Kanji Book: Learning Kanji the Fun and Easy Way!, Eriko and Anna Sato (Tuttle Shokai Inc., 2009)

Websites

www.enchantedlearning.com/themes/japan.shtml

library.thinkquest.org/CR0212302/japan.html

web-jpn.org/kidsweb/language

kids.asiasociety.org/explore/childrens-day-japan-kodomo-no-hi

Index